PAID IN FULL

YOUR DEBT

GOD'S PAYMENT

PAUL

CHAPPELL

First published in 2014 by Striving Together Publications, a
ministry of Lancaster Baptist Church, Lancaster, CA 93535. Striving
Together Publications is committed to providing tried, trusted, and
proven books that will further equip local churches to carry out the
Great Commission. Your comments and suggestions are valued.

Striving Together Publications
4020 E. Lancaster Blvd.
Lancaster, CA 93535
800.201.7748
strivingtogether.com

Cover design by Andrew Jones
Layout by Craig Parker
Writing assistance by Monica Bass
Special thanks to our proofreaders

ISBN 978-1-59894-278-1

Printed in the United States of America

CONTENTS

Paid in Love

There are many reasons we pay for things.

Sometimes we pay out of sheer responsibility. (Yes, electric company, I'm talking about you.)

Sometimes we pay out of a sense of obligation. (When your eight-year-old neighbor comes by to sell Girl Scout cookies, what kind of an ogre would you be to say no?)

Sometimes we pay out of selfishness. (We see; we want; we buy.)

But sometimes we pay out of love. These, of course, are the best purchases. They include the engagement ring you buy for the one you want to spend your life with. They include the "just because" gift you purchase for your mother or your child.

Gifts purchased out of love involve sacrifice and feeling. They are more than just "a thing"; they often represent blood, sweat, and tears. They are hard earned but freely given.

This little book is a story of the greatest gift in the history of the world—a gift purchased with the greatest love we will ever know. It is a gift purchased with the love *of God*. And it was purchased *for you*.

I don't know what you think of God. Or if you even believe in Him at all. But I do know that He loves you with a great love. And I know that He has purchased a gift for you—not out of responsibility, obligation, or selfishness—but out of love. It is a gift that required tremendous sacrifice—costly for Him, but freely offered to you.

Does this sound attractive to you? Do you struggle to believe it could be true? What if I told you that this gift is the gift of *eternal life?* A promised eternity in Heaven. A personal relationship with God. Eternal life.

Does it sound preposterous that this could be a *gift?* Everyone—at least everyone who believes in Heaven—knows that you have to *earn* Heaven, right? Or some people take a softer course—God is kind, and all roads lead to Heaven. Others reject the belief of Heaven outright. We are simply bodies, they say, and when our bodies die, that's the end.

But what if these theories are wrong? What if you are trying to earn a gift that has already been purchased? What if you are on a course that *doesn't* lead to Heaven? What if Heaven *is* real—and Hell is too?

What if there really is an incredible gift purchased by God—with your name on it? What if it was wrapped in the love of God and offered freely to you?

Would you be willing to explore with me what this gift is, how it was purchased, and why you and I so desperately need it?

This book is small because its message is simple. That is, it is simple to understand, but it is about profound love and grace. It is about the gift that cost God everything—a gift that is offered to *you.*

PART ONE

Your Debt

ONE

I Don't Know

They weren't the three words you would expect to hear from someone of his rank and stature in life—City Attorney for Los Angeles. We were sitting together at a lunch table, and the conversation turned to spiritual matters. I had asked him if he knew for sure if he would go to Heaven.

And then he spoke those three words: "I don't know."

Realize, we're talking about a man whose job it is to know things. If you're a prosecuting attorney, you study, learn, examine evidence, and come to solid conclusions. Then you present these conclusions in court and argue them with the strength of personal conviction of the facts and a commitment to see justice served.

And yet, when it came to life after death and where he would spend eternity, his answer was the same as I have heard not once, but thousands of times: "I don't know."

Of course, there are many variants of this phrase. Ask several people, "If you were to die, do you know for sure you would go to Heaven?" and you'll hear similar answers:

"I don't know."

"I hope so."

"I think so."

"Probably."

"I'm pretty good; I should go to Heaven."

"Maybe."

When I talked to my friend, who was at that time the City Attorney for Los Angeles, he hoped, too, he would go to Heaven. But like so many others, he wasn't sure, and he didn't know how to be sure.

Could we pretend for a moment that you and I are sitting across a lunch table? And could I ask you the same question I asked my friend, "Do you know for sure you'll spend eternity in Heaven?"

What You Don't Know *Can* Hurt You

You've heard the saying: "What you don't know can't hurt you." That may be true in a few situations, but it's surely not true when what you don't know involves the greatest questions of life and of life after death.

You see, we are more than a body; we have a spirit as well. That is, we have a part of us that has the ability to deeply communicate with other people and has the capacity to have a relationship with God. We have a spirit that will live somewhere forever—even after our body dies.

And that is why what we don't know *can* hurt us.

That is also why God has revealed the truth to us—the truth about His existence and about life after death and about the gift that He has provided for us. That is why God wants us to *know* the answers to life's greatest questions.

Jesus told us that knowing the truth will make us free: "And ye shall know the truth, and the truth shall make you free" (John 8:32).

What If You Could Know?

This is the question I asked my city attorney friend, "What if you could know your eternal future?"

Many people hope their good works, continual learning, open-mindedness, or sincere efforts are enough. And yet, God has promised us that we can know for sure that we have eternal life and a future home in Heaven.

You see, God does want us to know—not hope, but know. He even told us, "These things have I written unto you that believe on the name of the Son of God; **that ye may know that ye have eternal life,** and that ye may believe on the name of the Son of God" (1 John 5:13).

God does not want us to be left wondering about this important issue of eternal life. And so I ask you, would you like to *hope* about eternity? Or would you like to *know*?

TWO

Coming Up Short

You know that embarrassing feeling when you're standing at a checkout line digging in your pocket for sixty-five more cents?

I do—from experience. And every time it happens to me, I wish I didn't know the feeling.

Actually, I don't like the feeling of coming up short in any area. Who does?

And yet, all of us *do* come up short in a very significant way. Let me explain.

One-Word Diagnosis

To understand why all the uncertainty about eternity—why everyone doesn't automatically spend eternity with God—you have to understand a comprehensive diagnosis of the human race—a single word that describes us all.

If *you* could use just one word to describe yourself, what would it be?

Good? Kind? Well-meaning?

You probably are all of those.

Maybe today you're going through a tough season, and you'd use a different word.

Struggling? Lonely? Lost?

There are many words that could describe us all, but one of the words that describes every single person is not a word we like to own: *sinful.*

"But wait a minute!" you may say, "I'm not sinful! Sure, I'm not perfect, who is? I may come up a little short, but *sinful*? No way. I mean, I give to charity. I help my neighbor. I'm a caring parent and a loyal friend. I may struggle sometimes, but I'm definitely not *sinful!*"

Let me clarify. I use *sinful* in the sense that the Bible uses it. I'm not speaking only of the greatest, most awful acts of sin. I don't mean that you've robbed a bank, murdered someone, or are on the FBI's Most Wanted list. I also don't mean that you're alone—I'm sinful too.

Every honest person will acknowledge that he or she has done something wrong—that we are not perfect. The Bible verifies this in Ecclesiastes 7:20: "For there is not a just man upon earth, that doeth good, and sinneth not."

Romans 3:23 says it this way: "For all have sinned, and come short of the glory of God." Did you catch that phrase "come short of the glory of God"? We all know that we sometimes fall short. We don't always measure up to our expectations or to the demands life places upon us.

Sin, however, is a different kind of falling short. It's not simply bad judgment (like when you're short on change at the checkout) or human error (like forgetting an appointment). It is any action, thought, or motive that is against God's law. It can be something categorically criminal (like robbing a bank) or seemingly insignificant (like a white lie to look good to the boss).

And we *all* have done it. The best of us. The worst of us. You. Me. We have *all* sinned.

In the Beginning—a Choice

If it makes you feel any better, we came by our propensity to sin honestly. (Wow, is *that* an oxymoron!) You see we *inherited* a sin nature.

Go back with me several thousand years to the Garden of Eden. Perhaps you've heard of it and of our first parents—Adam and Eve—who lived there. The garden was perfection like we can't understand. Beautiful. Fruitful. Wonderful. And the best part of it was that Adam and Eve had a perfect relationship with God. They even walked with Him in "the cool of the day." How awesome is that?

You maybe know the story already, but if not, you can read about it in Genesis 3:1–7. I'll summarize here: God gave Adam and Eve the complete garden. They could enjoy and eat of any part of it—except for the fruit from one tree: the "tree of the knowledge of good and evil." What did Adam and Eve do? They ate of the one tree. And thus, the first sin was committed.

Remember, God had given Adam and Eve a choice. He could have kept them from the tree. He could have rendered them physically and emotionally incapable of sinning. But then they would be robots, not humans with a choice.

Having a choice meant that they were free to love or free to rebel. Even in this choice, they had everything in their favor: they knew God personally. They had the consequences of their choice clearly spelled out in advance. They were in a perfect environment.

And yet they still chose sin. And that choice has descended upon us all. Romans 5:12 explains it this way: "Wherefore, as by one man [Adam] sin entered into the world, and death by sin; and so death passed upon all men, for that all have sinned."

We'll see in our next chapter what the part "death by sin" means. But for now, consider that all of us, as descendants of Adam, are born with a "sin nature"—a bent toward doing wrong.

If you're a parent, this is not hard to understand. You never had to sit your toddler down and say, "Today, I'm going to teach you how to lie. If you do well, tomorrow we'll learn how to throw a tantrum. Maybe next week, I'll show you the best way to steal and hurt people." We don't teach our children how to sin—just as no one taught us. We're all born already knowing how.

Sin comes from *within* us. This is why God says that we are all sinful.

The Divine Measuring Stick

Maybe you admit that you aren't perfect—that you sometimes fall a little short—but you still hesitate to call yourself a "sinner." After all, you have good intentions and a kind heart, and compared to your neighbors, co-workers, or your mother-in-law (especially your mother-in-law), you're actually a very good person.

Enter the divine measuring stick—the law of God.

You see, we like to think of ourselves as being mostly good with occasional lapses of judgment. But since *we* are not the ones deciding our fate, we should look at *God's* standard. And He's given it to us throughout the Bible, perhaps most succinctly in what we call the "Ten Commandments."

There's something you should know about this measuring stick, though. Many people assume that if they keep the Ten Commandments, they've measured up to God's standard and are on their way to Heaven. This assumption is riddled with problems—not the least of which is that most people who believe this cannot even *name* the Ten Commandments, let alone *live* them.

But of even greater significance is that God never—not even once—told us that the way to get to Heaven is to obey all the commandments. On the contrary, He knows that we *can't* live up to His commandments. He didn't give them to us as a checklist, but as a mirror. He wants us to see our condition for what it is.

In other words, we may think we're doing pretty good until we look in the mirror of the Ten

Commandments and see "Thou shalt not bear false witness" and realize that we do—at least sometimes—lie. Then we realize we're not quite as faultless as we wanted to think.

In fact, if we look at all ten of these commandments—God's measuring stick—with honest transparency, we don't measure up. Not by a long shot. This is why God says we "come short of the glory of God."

Nobody likes to come up short, and so we find a way around it. We might compare ourselves to someone else. "Maybe I'm not perfect," we reason, "but at least I'm not as bad as _____."

This reminds me of the little boy who told his mother, "Mom! I'm six feet tall!" When she asked him how he came up with that height, he answered, "I used my shoe." His mom smiled and told him that his shoe was not a foot long. "But, Mom," he insisted, "it's got to be—'cause my foot's in it!"

Many people believe they are pretty good because they are using a faulty standard—comparing themselves to someone else.

Here's the problem with that reasoning: God is not comparing us to someone else. God is holy—absolutely free of sin. If He compared us to any standard other than Himself, He would no longer be holy, because every other person is sinful. He cannot be holy and compare us to an unholy standard.

Even if the *only* commandment we ever broke was one—say, stealing—we'd be in trouble. The Bible tells us, "For whosoever shall keep the whole law, and yet offend in one point, he is guilty of all" (James 2:10). Think of the law like a chain. If every link was sound—except for one—would you count on that chain to bear your weight? Of course not. If one link is broken, the whole chain is broken.

Why then would we count on our goodness to take us to Heaven, when we know that we are not *perfectly* good? To count on our goodness is like counting on a broken chain. If we are going to justify ourselves by the law, we have to be absolutely *perfect* in every point of the law.

But we're not perfect. We fall short. In another word, we are *sinners.*

Why You Need to Know This

If by now you're getting the picture that achieving God's standard of perfection is impossible, you're absolutely correct.

But there's more: God doesn't expect us to achieve perfection. He simply wants us to see ourselves for what we are—that way we can see His answer for what we need.

In fact, in a few pages we're going to see that acknowledging the fact that we are sinners actually brings some wonderfully good news. But before the good news, we have to understand one more thing about sin—its price tag.

THREE

Evaluating the Damage

Several years ago, I was driving with my wife and daughter in the car when the driver in front of us made a sudden left turn without moving into the left turn lane. It didn't help that I was in the middle of an intense phone conversation when it happened.

As the driver of the other vehicle and I got out to look at our cars, I was relieved to see it was just a fender bender.

My insurance adjuster, however, saw things a little differently. He called the accident a "liability," and he included increased insurance premiums in his evaluation of the damage.

In this chapter, we're going to look at the problem of sin a little like that adjuster. We're going to evaluate what the damage of sin actually is. After all, as people who do lots of good but sometimes sin, we can't be looking at too much damage, can we?

Minimum Costs

Everyone wants to get paid for what they do. Politicians argue endlessly on what the "minimum wage"—the lowest an employee can be paid by the hour—should be. And most people search for the job in which they will be paid the highest amount for their labor.

When it comes to payment for sin, however, the minimum wage is pretty steep. Romans 6:23 tells us, "For the wages of sin is death…."

Death!

Really? The payment for sin is *death?*

We already saw in Romans 5:12 that death came into the world by Adam's sin: "Wherefore, as by one man [Adam] sin entered into the world, *and death by sin….*" If you're familiar with the account of Adam and Eve eating the forbidden fruit, you'll remember two things: First, God did promise that death would be the consequence of sin (Genesis 2:17). Second, Adam and Eve did not keel over and die the moment they took a bite of the fruit.

So what is this death all about?

Separation

Death in the Bible refers to "separation." This is obvious to us all in the sense of physical death. When our bodies die, we are separated from our families and loved ones. If you've lost a loved one, you understand the separation pain of death.

But remember, you are more than a body. You have a spirit as well. The physical death that every person eventually experiences is the result of the fact that there is sin in the world. But, more personally, the *spiritual* death that you and I face is the result of our own sin.

Or we could say it this way: The payment of sin is eternal death—eternal separation from God—in a lake of fire that the Bible calls Hell: "And death and hell were cast into the lake of fire. This is the second death" (Revelation 20:14).

High Wages

These are high wages indeed! So much so that we are tempted to think them extreme. Many people even reason, "Surely a good God would not send people to Hell!"

And yet, this is absolutely what the Bible says. God tells us the wages—the payment—of sin is death and that this death includes eternal separation from God.

By our calculations, the wages of sin may be high, but remember, we are not the Judge. God is.

The story is told of a Jewish woman who was approached by a Christian friend about the matter of eternity. In the discussion her friend began to tell her of the payment for sin. She cried out, "I don't believe in Hell!"

"Why not?" asked the Christian friend.

"Because over six million of my Jewish brothers and sisters were murdered at the hands of Adolf Hitler and his Nazis. I cannot believe they will all go to Hell!"

Her friend then asked her, "So I suppose that when you get to Heaven and walk down the streets of gold, you'll see Adolf Hitler there. Will you tell him 'hello' for me?"

"Adolf Hitler!" she shouted. "Why, he won't be in Heaven, he'll be in Hell!"

Yes, even this woman saw that God is just to punish sinners. The difference was simply in her definition of who is sinful.

The truth is that we are all sinful—not on the scale of Hitler, but on the scale of God's law.

And the Bible tells us that because of our sin, we face eternity apart from God. What are we to do?

FOUR

Insufficient Payments

A Brooklyn man was once arrested for burglary and sentenced to several years in the state penitentiary. A few years into his sentence, the man escaped from prison and disappeared. Police detectives spent hours searching for him, following leads, and analyzing his escape, but to nò avail. Although many detectives gave up on the case after several years, one young detective never gave up. Bit by bit, he tracked down every clue and kept searching for the escapee until one day, many years later, he finally found the escaped criminal.

Following him to a convenience store, the detective approached him from behind, laid his hand on his shoulder, and notified him that he was under arrest. Shocked, the escapee said, "What'd I do, officer?"

"I know what you did years ago. I know how you broke out of prison, disappeared out west, got married, then came back to live with your family."

Realizing he would serve years in prison, the man asked the officer if they could at least go to his house so he could say goodbye to his family. Seeing the sorrow in his eyes, the officer agreed. When they arrived at his house, the man asked his wife, "Have I been a good husband to you? Have I been a good father to our children?"

"Why yes," replied the wife, "you have. But why are you asking me this?"

At that point the escaped man explained everything to his wife, relaying past events he thought would stay hidden. He begged the detective to recognize how he had turned his life around and to pardon him, yet the detective still handcuffed him and led him away.

We read a story such as this, and we immediately understand the futility of an escaped criminal using his current behavior to erase his guilty record. As upstanding as he may have been in the moment, he was still guilty of burglary and had not finished his sentence.

Even so, people today make similar—although even more futile—attempts as that burglar. Although many people have not specifically considered what the Bible says is the wages of sin (eternal death), we all intuitively know that we come up short in some way, and so we try to make up the difference by goodness in another way. Consider these methods:

Religion

After all, religion is made for reaching God, right? Surely this is the way to Heaven!

Religious systems may seem logical, but they cannot pay the debt created by our sin. God declared that the payment for sin is death—not church membership, catechism, giving money, daily prayers, or any other "installments" we may try to make via religion.

Many people actually use religion as a fashionable substitute for biblical belief. One such man was Nicodemus, and you can read his story in John 3. In short, Nicodemus was not only religious, he was the picture of religion—a leader, a conscientious follower, a good man. But when he came to Jesus one night and asked Jesus how he could know he had eternal life, Jesus told Nicodemus that his religion wasn't enough. It didn't even tip the scale. Jesus told him he had to be "born again."

No, religion won't pay the debt created by sin. It's insufficient.

Good Works

Being a good neighbor, volunteering for community service projects, giving to the poor, and loving and nurturing your family are all excellent ways to invest your time. But the Bible tells us plainly that none of these are payment for sin. Ephesians 2:9 says that eternal life is "Not of works, lest any man should boast." If we could earn our way to Heaven by our good works, we'd get there with another layer of sin—pride in what we did!

Actually, even our good works are tainted by our sinfulness. That's why the Bible says "…and all our righteousnesses are as filthy rags…" (Isaiah 64:6). This is not hyperbole; it is a real comparison. Our good works may look good when we compare them to another person's, but they are unclean when compared to God's holiness.

Money

Some people try to buy their way into Heaven. Whether that be by giving to a church or to a charity, they hope God will see their sacrifice and let them in. Former mayor of New York City, Michael Bloomberg, famously gave $50 million to a cause he believed in and commented, "I am telling you if there is a God, when I get to Heaven I'm not stopping to be interviewed. I am heading straight in. I have earned my place in Heaven. It's not even close."[1]

Actually, the mayor is only partially right. He was right that "it's not even close," but that is because money can *never* buy Heaven. The Bible tells us that redemption—having our sin paid for—can't be bought "with corruptible things, as silver and gold" (1 Peter 1:18).

In all honesty, can you imagine what one moment in Heaven would cost if it could be bought with money? Considering that several years ago someone paid $351,000 just to have lunch with Warren Buffet, I don't think Mr. Bloomberg could even buy a vacation in Heaven.[2] All the money in the world is insufficient as a payment for Heaven because money cannot atone for sin.

Self-Inflicted Punishment

I've watched people climb the steps to St. Peter's Basilica in Rome on their hands and knees until their skin was scraped, torn, and bleeding. I've read the accounts of people in the Philippines who ask to be crucified as Christ was in an attempt to pay for their sins. Some who don't torture themselves in this life believe that purgatory will do it in the next.

Here's the thing: *if* self-crucifixion—or any other form of torture—could earn a place in Heaven, it would be worth it. But not only is it unnecessary pain, it is pointless. The wages of sin is not pain, it is death, eternal separation from God.

Sincerity

You've heard the statement: "All roads lead to the same place." Many people assume that as long as they are sincere and believe in God, they're on their way— perhaps on a different way than others, but on their way nonetheless—to Heaven.

This is one of the most popular theories in our pluralistic day. It sounds noble and broad-minded. In fact, saying otherwise seems to many people to be backwards and narrow-minded.

One problem: God said otherwise. Proverbs 14:12 says, "There is a way which seemeth right unto a man, but the end thereof are the ways of death." In other words, it's not what seems right to us that matters. It's not our sincerity that will gain us entrance into Heaven—for we can be sincerely wrong!

Jesus was very plain when He said, "I am the way, the truth, and the life: no man cometh unto the Father, but by me" (John 14:6). We'll look at this verse again in a little bit, but for now, notice that Jesus said there is just one acceptable way to God.

Acceptable Payments

What you use to pay for something matters. For instance, I can't pay my mortgage debt in exchange for baking thousands of cookies. (Although I would try it if I thought it might work.) I can't pay it by telling my banker I'll mow his lawn every week for twenty years or that I'll use my home to house poor, orphaned children. The only acceptable payment for my mortgage debt is cash.

Similarly, we can't pay our sin debt through religion, good works, money, self-punishment, sincerity, or any other method. The only acceptable payment has already been set by God, and it is death. Regardless of our sincerity, it's not what *we* think will gain us entrance into Heaven that counts. It is what *God* says that matters. But more than what God says, it is what God *did* that makes all the difference in the world!

Where Grace Steps In

It is only when we understand our sin and the severe—but just—penalty that God has placed on sin that we understand the greatness of God's love.

You and I are sinners. There's no way around that fact. As 1 John 1:8 says, "If we say that we have no sin, we deceive ourselves, and the truth is not in us." If you deny it, make up your own answers for how you think God should deal with it, or try to pay for it yourself, you will be making futile and insufficient payments toward a tremendous debt.

If, on the other hand, you see your sin for what it is—a separation between you and God that makes you fall short of His glory—you're beginning to get an accurate picture of your helpless condition.

This is exactly where God's amazing grace steps in. Jesus said, "They that are whole have no need of the physician, but they that are sick: I came not to call the righteous, but sinners to repentance" (Mark 2:17).

To those who think they have it all together or who assume their method of paying for their sin is enough, God's grace seems unnecessary. It's like a person who goes to the doctor. The doctor tells him he has a large cancerous tumor, but the person insists he doesn't. That person isn't likely to follow the treatment plan the doctor may prescribe because he doesn't even realize how sick he is! Similarly, if we think we're okay on our own—that we don't have sin or that we can deal with it our own way—we won't see how desperately we need God's grace. And I'm not just talking about God's grace in general; I'm talking about a specific, tangible way that God demonstrated His grace to us.

Read this next verse slowly; it is a *game changer:* "But God commendeth [showed] his love toward us, in that, *while we were yet sinners, Christ died for us*" (Romans 5:8).

Did you catch that? Jesus didn't die for those who could earn salvation on their own (and remember, none of us can). He died for sinners. Sinners like me. Like you.

There is only one truly unconditional love in the world—and it is God's. Although we are sinners separated from Him, He still loved us. And that love is not merely a nice sentiment—God feeling kindly toward us. It is real and powerful, and it prompted unbelievable sacrifice.

Remember I told you there was some good news coming? That good news is what we'll see in our next chapter.

If you're ready for the good news, turn the page. You're about to discover the gift God wants to give you.

PART TWO

God's Payment

FIVE

Substitute Payment

Some years ago, a well-known Bible preacher was pulled over for speeding in a small southern town and taken to traffic court. The preacher pleaded guilty because he had been speeding. He knew he would have to pay a fine for speeding, and sure enough, the judge pronounced him guilty and stated the fine.

But the preacher didn't expect what happened next.

Suddenly, the judge recognized the preacher, and he didn't want to fine him. He wouldn't be a just judge, however, if he simply said, "Yeah, you're guilty, but because you're famous, you can go free."

Instead, the judge reached into his pocket and pulled out the amount of the fine. "You're guilty," he said, "and the fine must be paid. But I'm going to pay it for you."

This is a very small picture of what Jesus did for us when He died. We are guilty of sin. The payment is death. And Jesus *died for us.*

Did you catch that? The Judge Himself came to Earth to pay the price of our sin. He died in *our* place. He made Himself the substitute payment for our sin. Let me explain.

Jesus Came for This

To understand Jesus' substitute payment, there is something else you must understand: Jesus is God. He didn't just claim to be God (although He did claim that[1]); He actually is *in fact* God.

Why is this important? Because if Jesus is just another human—even a *good* human—His death can't be a substitute for our death. He would be paying for His own sin—not ours.

Think about it this way. Let's say that I was a convicted criminal on death row, sentenced to be executed tomorrow morning. Suppose you and I are dear friends and you voluntarily ask the judge to allow you to die in my place.

In some judicial systems, this would be allowed— an innocent person can take the punishment of a guilty person while the guilty person goes free.

But let's say that you were also a condemned criminal on death row. There is no way the judge could allow you to die in *my* place; you are already sentenced to die for *your* crimes.

The only reason Christ's payment could be a substitute for our punishment is because Christ never sinned—He is God. And the only reason that Christ's payment can be a substitute for *everybody's* sin is because, as God, Christ is infinite. His payment is enough for the sin of every person in the world.

Jesus came as God in the flesh to reveal to us who God is and to suffer for our sin. The Bible says, "God was manifest in the flesh..." (1 Timothy 3:16). That's talking about Jesus. John 1:1 and 14 says of Jesus, "In the beginning was the Word, and the Word was with God, and the Word was God…. And the Word was made flesh, and dwelt among us, (and we beheld his glory, the glory as of the only begotten of the Father,) full of grace and truth."

Jesus is God, and when He came to pay for our sins, He came as a just Judge who can't overlook sin—but paid for it Himself.

Costly Payment

Jesus was supernaturally conceived of a virgin[2] and humbled Himself to be born as a helpless infant living in an earthly family.[3] At the age of thirty, He began His public ministry—healing the sick, curing the lame, cleansing lepers, and even raising a few dead. If you had lived in the first century and were an intellectually honest and unbiased observer of Jesus' miracles (especially raising the dead miracles), you'd have to acknowledge that this was no ordinary man. Surely this was God. In fact, the miracles did prove His deity.

To make a long story short, after three years of preaching, teaching, and performing miracles, the jealous religious leaders of Jesus' day were finally successful in having Jesus condemned to the horrific death of crucifixion.

What Jesus voluntarily[4] endured at His crucifixion is the supreme evidence of the love of God. (You can read a full account of this event—from four different perspectives—in Matthew 27, Mark 15, Luke 23, and John 19.)

First, Christ was scourged—fiercely whipped with a Roman flagrum until it was a marvel that He still lived. Other victims had died from the scourging alone.

Next, Jesus was led to the judgment hall, where Roman soldiers mocked Him as "King of the Jews" and further tortured Him by placing a crown of thorns on His head and driving it into His skull.

Jesus was then forced to carry His cross. When He stumbled under it, weakened from loss of blood, the soldiers made a bystander carry it for Him.

And then they got to Calvary, the place of crucifixion. They nailed Jesus' hands and feet to the cross. They lifted the cross and dropped it into place, no doubt causing Jesus' body to jerk and tear the flesh while dislocating his arms from the shoulder sockets. The searing pain of this moment was so terrible that crucifixion victims often fainted.

For six hours, Jesus hung on the cross, suspended between Heaven and Earth in unspeakable pain and unbelievable sacrifice.

For crucifixion victims who lived through the scourging and the crucifixion itself, Roman soldiers would sometimes end their lives by breaking their legs so they could no longer lift themselves up to breathe. But when the soldiers came to break Christ's legs, they found He had already died. (This, like every other aspect of Christ's crucifixion, fulfilled prophecies and sacrificial requirements given by God hundreds of years before Jesus came to earth. Of this moment, John 19:36 says, "For these things were done, that the scripture should be fulfilled, A bone of him shall not be broken.") Just to be sure Jesus was dead, the soldiers rammed a spear through His side. Water and blood flowed from the gaping wound. Jesus had died.

Paid in Full

Just before Jesus died, He uttered three final words: "It is finished" (John 19:30).

"It is finished."

What did those words mean? How could Jesus say "It is finished"? There were still sick and unbelieving people in the world. There were still people who were lame and blind and suffering.

What was finished?

The Greek word Jesus used that is translated *finished* in our English Bible is *tetelestai.* It is a financial term that means "paid in full."

Paid in full!

Remember what God says the wages of sin is? "The wages of sin is death" (Romans 6:23). And so what did Jesus do? "But God commendeth his love toward us, in that, while we were yet sinners, *Christ died for us*" (Romans 5:8).

The wages of sin is *death;* Jesus *died* for us. *Literally,* He paid our debt for sin.

And, as God, He paid it in full.

Proof

Three days after Jesus was crucified and buried, He—and let this sink in—*rose from the dead.* Jesus didn't just *say* "It is finished"; He *proved* it by His resurrection.

The resurrection of Jesus Christ is, as one man put it, "the crowning proof of Christianity."[5] He didn't rise from the dead quietly or without anyone knowing. In the Bible, there are over ten different recorded appearances of Jesus after He rose from the dead.[6] He showed Himself multiple times—one of which was to over five hundred gathered at once who testified as eye witnesses.[7]

So what does all of this mean for you—right now, today?

Satisfactory Payment

In the previous chapter, we saw *insufficient* payments. The one thing all of those payments have in common is that they involve our work or personal effort. In all of those payments—religion, good works, money, self-inflicted punishment, sincerity in our beliefs—there is some way that we are attempting to pay for our sin.

In fact, at the heart of every religion around the world is the idea that we are supposed to *do* something. What that something is varies from one religion to the next. It may be saying a certain prayer or saying it enough times. It may be giving money to the church. It may be baptism, meditation, or acts of kindness.

But at the heart of it all is the same philosophy: *do. You have to do something to pay for your sin.*

Work.

Try harder.

Earn forgiveness.

The problem with this plan is that anything that we might *do* is an insufficient payment. So where does that leave us?

In contrast to all of our systems of working, Jesus offers another option—the only option that could ever work: full, complete forgiveness for sin through what He has already paid for at the cross.

Religion says *do;* Jesus says *done.*

We say *try harder;* Jesus says *paid in full.*

It is finished.

Paid in full.

Do you want this payment applied to your account? That's where we pick up in our next chapter.

SIX

Forgiven

Outside New York City is a cemetery with one unique grave marker. On the headstone is carved a single word: FORGIVEN. There is no name and no date of birth or date of death on the stone. There is no ornamentation and no epitaph offering wisdom or advice. But in that single word, there is peace and certain hope that is beyond price.

You see, God's forgiveness is available to all of us.

Our natural thinking is that good people go to Heaven. But God says, "There is none righteous, no, not one" (Romans 3:10).

The wonderful truth is that it is not *good* people who go to Heaven; it is *forgiven* people.

If we try to get to Heaven on our merit, we're sunk. Because even if from this moment forward you were *perfect*—without even a hint of sin—there is still the fact that you have already sinned, and that every sin must be dealt with. As we have seen, the payment for sin is death.

So Jesus stepped in and took our payment for us so we could be—not *good*—but *forgiven.*

In an incredibly divine deal, God offers to declare you forgiven and righteous. Sound incredible? It is! But it's also real—an offer based on the radical love of God and the incredible sacrifice He made on the cross.

Here's how it works: "For he [God] hath made him [God the Son—Jesus] to be sin for us, who knew no sin; that we might be made the righteousness of God in him" (2 Corinthians 5:21).

It really is that simple. Jesus paid for your sin and is willing to give you His righteousness.

It Is a Gift

Jesus' payment for sin is why eternal life is—and only ever can be—a gift. Earlier we saw from Romans 6:23 that "the wages of sin is death," but that is only the first half of the verse! The second half says, "but the *gift of God* is eternal life through Jesus Christ our Lord."

You see, salvation—or eternal life—is not something we *achieve;* it is something we *receive.*

An Inclusive Offer

It's the most well-known verse in the entire Bible: John 3:16. And it summarizes everything we've seen already. "For God so loved the world, that he gave his only begotten Son, that *whosoever* believeth in him should not perish, but have everlasting life."

Did you notice the word I emphasized? Whosoever.

That means anybody. It is the most inclusive word in the entire Bible—and it includes *you!*

An Exclusive Offer

This offer of forgiveness is *inclusive*, a personal offer to you. But it is also *exclusive*—available *only* through Jesus Christ.

Some people like to think that by dying on the cross, Jesus opened the way to Heaven—as in, He now made it possible for us to earn our way there.

Others like to think that they are trusting Jesus *and* other religions, philosophies, or themselves. They say things like, "Sure, I'm trusting in Jesus—*and* Buddhism" or "*and* positive thinking," "*and* baptism," "*and…*". Or they use the old quip "All roads lead to Rome" and assume that all roads lead to Heaven as well.

This sort of thinking may be popular, but it is the opposite of what Jesus said: "I am the way, the truth, and the life: no man cometh unto the Father, but by me" (John 14:6).

In another place, the Bible says of Jesus, "Neither is there salvation in any other: for there is none other name under heaven given among men, whereby we must be saved" (Acts 4:12).

You see, Jesus isn't just *a* way to Heaven; He is *the* way to Heaven. He is the only One who could pay for our sins and then offer us full and complete forgiveness as a gift.

Don't Refuse Your Pardon

In 1829, two men, George Wilson and James Porter, were convicted of robbing the U.S. Mail and endangering the life of a postal driver in the process. Porter was executed, but Wilson's execution was delayed as friends pleaded on his behalf.

In June of 1830, President Andrew Jackson issued a full pardon to Wilson, allowing him to go free. Strangely, however, Wilson refused to avail himself of the pardon.

Ultimately, the Supreme Court was called on to decide Wilson's fate. Chief Justice John Marshall delivered the court's ruling, including the statement: "A pardon is a deed...and if it be rejected, we have discovered no power in a court to force it on him."[1]

Although Wilson was offered forgiveness, he rejected it.

Don't make the same mistake. Jesus offers you forgiveness—which He obtained at great cost. Don't reject it. Receive it!

SEVEN

Believe It, Receive It

Several years ago, the Consumer Reports National Research Center reported that one out of five gift card recipients never used their cards, representing about $972 million—almost $1 billion—in unredeemed cards.[1]

Why? Here were the reasons the gift card owners reported:

- Didn't have time: 50 percent
- Didn't find anything they wanted: 37 percent
- Lost the card: 14 percent
- Card expired: 12 percent

These gift cards, regardless of the value on the card, did the gift recipients no good. To be sure, the money was available—already loaded on the card. But without using the card, the money made no difference to the person who received it.

Similarly, Jesus already paid for our sins on the cross. But the fact of His atonement is not enough. We must apply it to our lives by simple faith.

There is a difference between knowing something and having faith in it. In fact, the Bible tells us that even "the devils also believe, and tremble" (James 2:19).

Knowing Jesus paid for your sin in full and *trusting* His payment is like the difference between *having* a gift card and *using* that gift card.

Believe It

Of course, to receive something, you have to believe it is real—a genuine offer. If I offer to give you a geographic landmark, such as the Eiffel Tower, you might say, "Sure, thanks." But you would just be saying that to be kind. Mentally, you'd be considering the possibility that I needed serious help!

To receive the gift of eternal life, you must believe that it is a real offer—that what God has said about it is true.

Let's recap. In these pages, we've seen from the Bible the following truths:

All of us have sinned.

> For all have sinned, and come short of the glory of God;—ROMANS 3:23

This sin separates us from God, and it has the price tag of death—in Hell, eternally separated from God.

> For the wages of sin is death…—ROMANS 6:23

But Christ died for our sin. He paid the final and complete price.

> But God commendeth his love toward us, in that, while we were yet sinners, Christ died for us.—ROMANS 5:8

And we must trust in Christ exclusively for salvation.

> Neither is there salvation in any other: for there is none other name under heaven given among men, whereby we must be saved.
> —Acts 4:12

> ...the gift of God is eternal life through Jesus Christ our Lord.—Romans 6:23

Jesus paid our price in full so we wouldn't have to. He offers this salvation from sin to you as a gift. Your choice to receive it or reject it is the difference between Heaven and Hell, between eternal life and eternal death.

Receive Christ by Faith

To receive the gift of an eternal home in Heaven, we must stop trusting ourselves, our works, or our religion and place our full trust in Jesus Christ alone for the forgiveness of our sin and eternal life.

Think of these three words: *call, turn, trust.*

You *call* out to the Lord for His gift. You *turn* from self-effort. And you *trust* the payment Jesus already made. In the language of the Bible this is "repentance toward God [turning from self], and faith toward our

Lord Jesus Christ [trusting what He has done on your behalf]" (Acts 20:21).

In Romans 10:13 the Bible says, "For whosoever shall call upon the name of the Lord shall be saved." That is a promise directly from God that if you will pray to Him, confess that you are a sinner, and ask Him to forgive your sins, turning to Him alone to be your Saviour, He will give you eternal life.

The Bible isn't talking here about "praying all the time" or deciding to be a religious person. It is speaking of a definitive decision to forsake previous assumptions and turn away from your efforts for salvation, choosing to trust only in what Jesus did to pay for your sins.

The phrase "call upon the name of the Lord" brings to mind an image of someone drowning, stranded far out in the ocean with no way to make it to shore. Picture yourself as that person—hopeless and helpless.

But then an ocean liner appears on the scene. You wave your arms high and call out for help. When the ship comes to you and throws out a lifeboat, would you say, "Aw, thanks! But I'm okay. I'll just keep swimming here as long as I know you're nearby"? No! You're going to throw yourself into that lifeboat—it's your only hope of salvation.

Similarly, the Bible tells us we are lost in sin. Without Jesus' sacrifice on our behalf, we will die and spend eternity in Hell, separated from God. But if we call out to Him—"call upon the name of the Lord"— for salvation, He promises He will save us.

In Romans 10:9–10 God tells us we have simply to call out for salvation—believing the truth about who Jesus is in our hearts—and we will be saved: "That if thou shalt confess with thy mouth the Lord Jesus, and shalt believe in thine heart that God hath raised him from the dead, thou shalt be saved. For with the heart man believeth unto righteousness; and with the mouth confession is made unto salvation."

It's as simple as believing what God says and then choosing to call out to Him for salvation. You can make the decision today to receive God's gift by praying from your heart something like this:

> Dear Lord, I know that I am a sinner. I confess that in my sin, I cannot save myself. Right now,

> I turn to You alone to be my Saviour. I ask you to save me from the penalty of my sin, and I receive Your gift of eternal life.—Amen

If you just now made the decision to receive Christ as your Saviour, allow me to be the first to congratulate you! In over five decades of life, I can unreservedly and with zero hesitation tell you that this was the greatest decision I ever made.

And what's more, receiving the gift of eternal life isn't the *end* of the gift—it's just the *beginning!* Eternal life is not only a joy to *receive;* it is a joy to *own.* In fact, the more you understand the enormity of what this gift is and the better you get to know the One who gave it to you, the more wonderful it is!

Now You Know

Remember at the beginning of this little book when we saw that God wants us to *know* that we have eternal life? Remember my City Attorney friend who didn't know? The good news is that he *did* choose to trust Christ as his Saviour. He, like so many others have done, called upon the name of the Lord to be saved.

If you also just "called upon the name of the Lord," you have the promise from God that you are saved! He didn't say, "whosoever shall call upon the name of the Lord *might* be saved." He said, "whosoever shall call upon the name of the Lord **shall** be saved."

Look again at the verse that we saw in chapter 1: "These things have I written unto you that believe on the name of the Son of God; *that ye may know that ye have eternal life,* and that ye may believe on the name of the Son of God" (1 John 5:13). It is through believing on Jesus that we have God's promise of eternal life and the confidence that we *know* we have it!

In man's ideas of getting salvation by our works, we can never *know for sure* that we have eternal life. We're left hoping and trying and wondering. But in God's perfect plan, salvation is sure. We receive God's gift, and we know He will keep His promise.

And the best of it is, God's promises are always good—you can take them to the bank!

EIGHT

Take It to the Bank

Have you ever taken a bad check to the bank? Someone gave you a check indicating they had money in their account to cover it, but when you attempted to cash or deposit the check, it bounced?

Or has someone ever made you a bad promise? They told you something they would do, but when the time came, they abandoned their promise? There are some people you just can't really trust anything they say.

With God, it's the opposite. When He gives a promise, you can rest in full confidence that He will keep it! Including when He promises eternal life.

If you have just received God's gift of eternal life, I want to take these last few pages to encourage you in understanding just how secure this gift really is. In other words, I want you to know that when God gives a gift, it's for keeps!

Secure Promises

I've read that the most impenetrable bank vault in the world is Fort Knox—the United States bullion depository. If a robber were to somehow get through the solid granite wall perimeter and pass the squadrons of machine gun-wielding guards and armed military, the thief would still have to contend with a twenty-two-ton vault door. That door is held shut by a lock so intricate that it requires a ten-person team to unlock it.[1] If you're looking for easy cash, you're definitely not going to find it at Fort Knox.

The gift that God has given you of eternal life is even more secure than the bullion stored at Fort Knox. Jesus explained it this way: "And I give unto them eternal life; and they shall never perish, neither shall any man pluck them out of my hand. My Father, which gave them me, is greater than all; and no man is able to pluck them out of my Father's hand" (John 10:28–29).

Jesus promised to give *eternal* life to anyone who calls out to Him for salvation. By definition, *eternal* life can never end or be taken away. But to emphasize the security of this promise, Jesus painted a picture for us. He said He holds us tightly in His hand. And the Father's hand is wrapped around even Jesus' hand!

Talk about security! Fort Knox has nothing on the hand of God.

You Can't Lose It

Some people who trust Jesus to be their Saviour begin to worry that maybe something they do wrong will make them lose the promise of eternal life. Even though they know God promises to keep them secure, they are concerned that if they sin they will forfeit their salvation.

If you feel this fear, I have good news for you! You may be able to lose money, but you can't lose your salvation.

Since we cannot earn salvation by anything we do, we cannot lose it by what we do (or don't do) either. The blood of Jesus stands as our continual payment for sin. First John 1:7 says, "…the blood of Jesus Christ his Son cleanseth us from *all* sin."

Just a few verses later—to really nail it down—the Bible continues, "My little children, these things write I unto you, that ye sin not. And if any man sin, we have an advocate with the Father, Jesus Christ the righteous: And he is the propitiation [meaning *covering*] for our sins…" (1 John 2:1–2).

These verses admonish us not to just keep sinning without caring, but they also acknowledge that we do, in fact, still sin sometimes. And when we do, we know that we are still secure in the payment Jesus made for us.

The certainty of God's promises and the security of our salvation are woven all throughout the Bible in multitudes of direct references and poignant analogies. For instance, God uses the analogy of sonship—that those who have trusted Christ are now God's sons and daughters.[2] He even likens salvation to a new birth.[3] Just as you cannot biologically change the family into which you were physically born, when you become God's child through a spiritual birth (by asking Jesus to be your Saviour), you are forever His son or daughter. He will never disown or expel you from the family.

It's for Real

If you were to decide to purchase a house today, you would likely need to call a banker and work out a mortgage plan in which you would pay for the house over a period of years. But most lenders (except maybe your mother—maybe) aren't just going to take your word on the payments and give you the key to the house. They will ask you for "earnest money"—a large up-front sum to prove you are serious about the purchase.

Well, when it comes to our salvation, God voluntarily gave us an earnest to assure us that He is going to follow through on His promise of giving us a home in Heaven. And you'd better be sitting down before you read next what that earnest is.

It is God Himself.

The Holy Spirit—the third Person of the trinity—takes up residence in us the moment we trust Christ as Saviour. The Bible says that God has "given the earnest of the Spirit in our hearts" (2 Corinthians 1:22[4]).

If you received the gift of salvation, you also have the continual presence of God. The Holy Spirit will never leave us. Ever.

Rest in God's Promise

In all of these promises, we know that God absolutely does not—indeed, *cannot*—lie. Titus 1:2 says, "In hope [meaning *confidence*] of eternal life, which God, that cannot lie, promised before the world began."

Bank accounts run empty, and human guarantees fail. But God's promises are always sound! When God says, "If you call to Me for salvation, I will give you eternal life," you can rest in that promise.

Your gift is secure.

FINAL NOTE FROM THE AUTHOR

If you received the gift of God while reading this little book, I would love to hear from you and would like to send you a gift copy of God's Word and another small book titled *First Steps for New Christians* that will help you grow in your relationship with the Lord.

Simply contact Striving Together Publications with your name and mailing address so we can send you these gifts. May God bless you in your new relationship with Him!

EMAIL   paidinfull@strivingtogether.com

CALL   800.201.7748

WRITE   Striving Together Publications
4020 E. Lancaster Blvd.
Lancaster, CA 93535

NOTES

Chapter Four

1. Cheryl K. Chumley, "Michael Bloomberg: I've earned my place in Heaven for anti-gun crusade" (The Washington Times, April 16, 2014), http://www. washingtontimes.com/news/2014/apr/16/michael-bloomberg-ive-earned-my-place-in-heaven-fo/.
2. Bloomberg Businessweek, June 8, 2006.

Chapter Five

1. Matthew 9:2–6; John 10:30–33; John 20:28
2. Luke 1:35
3. Luke 2:7

4. Isaiah 50:6; Romans 5:6–8

5. Henry M. Morris, *Many Infallible Proofs: Evidences for the Christian Faith* (New Leaf Publishing Group, 1974) 97.

6. See John 20:11–18; Matthew 28:1–10; 1 Corinthians 15:5; Luke 24:13–35; John 20:19–24, 26–28, 21:1–23; 1 Corinthians 15:6–7; Acts 1:3–10, 9:3–9.

7. Acts 1:3; 1 Corinthians 15:6

Chapter Six

1. Legal Information Institute, "United States v. George Wilson" (accessed September 22, 2014), http://www.law. cornell.edu/supremecourt/text/32/150.

Chapter Seven

1. Jae Yang and Adrienne Lewis, "Americans Neglect a Billion in Gift Cards" (USA Today, November 20, 2006).

Chapter Eight

1. CMI Gold and Silver, "15 Most Impenetrable Bank Vaults," December 16, 2010, http://www.cmi-gold-silver. com/blog/15-impenetrable-bank-vaults/.

2. John 1:12; Romans 8:14

3. John 3; 2 Corinthians 5:17

4. See also 2 Corinthians 5:5 and Ephesians 1:13–14.

PAUL CHAPPELL is the senior pastor of Lancaster Baptist Church and president of West Coast Baptist College in Lancaster, California. His preaching is heard on Daily in the Word, a daily radio broadcast aired across America. Pastor Chappell has been married to his wife Terrie for over thirty-three years, and they have four married children and six grandchildren.

You can connect with Dr. Chappell through his blog, Twitter, and Facebook:

paulchappell.com
twitter.com/paulchappell
facebook.com/pastor.paul.chappell

For more information about our ministry visit the following websites:

strivingtogether.com
for helpful Christian resources

dailyintheword.org/today
for an encouraging word each day